BRITISH MUSEUM.

The Book of the Dead

WITH TWENTY-FIVE ILLUSTRATIONS.

I0102013

by British Museum

ISBN: 978-1-63923-601-5

Printed: January 2023

Published and Distributed By:
Lushena Books
607 Country Club Drive, Unit E
Bensenville, IL 60106
www.lushenabks.com

ISBN: 978-1-63923-601-5

THE BOOK OF THE DEAD.

I.

THE TITLE.

" BOOK OF THE DEAD " is the title now commonly given to the great collection of funerary texts which the ancient Egyptian scribes composed for the benefit of the dead. These consist of spells and incantations, hymns and litanies, magical formulae and names, words of power and prayers, and they are found cut or painted on walls of pyramids and tombs, and painted on coffins and sarcophagi and rolls of papyri. The title " Book of the Dead " is somewhat unsatisfactory and misleading, for the texts neither form a connected work nor belong to one period ; they are miscellaneous in character, and tell us nothing about the lives and works of the dead with whom they were buried. Moreover, the Egyptians possessed many funerary works that might rightly be called " Books of the Dead," but none of them bore a name that could be translated by the title " Book of the Dead." This title was given to the great collection of funerary texts in the first quarter of the nineteenth century by the pioneer Egyptologists, who possessed no exact knowledge of their contents. They were familiar with the rolls of papyrus inscribed in the hieroglyphic and the hieratic character, for copies of several had been published,[1] but the texts in them were short and fragmentary. The publication of the Facsimile[2] of the Papyrus of Peṭa-Ȧmen-neb-nest-taui[3] by

---

[1] See *Journal de Trévoux*, June, 1704 ; Caylus, *Antiq. Egypt.*, tom. I, plate 21 ; Denon, *Travels*, plates 136 and 137 ; and *Description de l'Égypte*, tom. II, plate 64 ff.

[2] *Copie Figurée d'un Rouleau de Papyrus trouvé à Thèbes dans un tombeau des Rois*. Paris, XIII–1805. This papyrus is nearly 30 feet in length and was brought to Strassburg by a paymaster in Napoleon's Army in Egypt called Poussielgue, who sold it to M. Cadet.

[3] .

A

M. Cadet in 1805 made a long hieroglyphic text and numerous coloured vignettes available for study, and the French Egyptologists described it as a copy of the " Rituel Funéraire " of the ancient Egyptians. Among these was Champollion le Jeune, but later, on his return from Egypt, he and others called it " Le Livre des Morts," " The Book of the Dead," " Das Todtenbuch," etc. These titles are merely translations of the name given by the Egyptian tomb-robbers to every roll of inscribed papyrus which they found with mummies, namely, " Kitâb al-Mayyit," " Book of the dead man," or " Kitâb al-Mayyitun," " Book of the dead " (plur.). These men knew nothing of the contents of such a roll, and all they meant to say was that it was " a dead man's book," and that it was found in his coffin with him.

II.

The Preservation of the Mummified Body in the Tomb by Thoth.

The objects found in the graves of the predynastic Egyptians, i.e., vessels of food, flint knives and other weapons, etc., prove that these early dwellers in the Nile Valley believed in some kind of a future existence. But as the art of writing was unknown to them their graves contain no inscriptions, and we can only infer from texts of the dynastic period what their ideas about the Other World were. It is clear that they did not consider it of great importance to preserve the dead body in as complete and perfect state as possible, for in many of their graves the heads, hands and feet have been found severed from the trunks and lying at some distance from them. On the other hand, the dynastic Egyptians, either as the result of a difference in religious belief, or under the influence of invaders who had settled in their country, attached supreme importance to the preservation and integrity of the dead body, and they adopted every means known to them to prevent its dismemberment and decay. They cleansed it and embalmed it with drugs, spices and balsams ; they anointed it with aromatic oils and preservative fluids ; they swathed it in hundreds of yards of linen bandages ; and then they sealed it up in a coffin or sarcophagus, which they laid in a chamber hewn in the bowels of the mountain. All these things were done to protect the physical body against damp, dry rot and decay, and against the attacks of moth, beetles, worms and wild animals. But these were not the only enemies of the dead against which precautions had to be taken, for both the mummified body and the spiritual elements which had inhabited it upon earth had to be protected from a multitude of devils and fiends, and from the powers of darkness generally. These powers of evil had hideous and terrifying shapes and forms, and their haunts were well known, for they infested the region through which the road of the dead lay when passing from this world to the Kingdom of Osiris. The "great gods" were afraid of them, and were obliged to protect themselves by the use of spells and magical names, and words of power, which were composed and written down by Thoth. In fact it was believed in very early times in Egypt that Rā the Sun-god owed his continued existence to the possession of a secret name with which Thoth had provided him. And each morning the rising sun was menaced by a fearful monster called Āapep, ☰ ꙮ, which lay hidden under the place of sunrise waiting to swallow up the solar disk. It was impossible, even for the Sun-god, to destroy this "Great Devil," but by reciting each morning the powerful spell with which

The Spearing of Āapep.
(*From the Papyrus of Nekhtu-Āmen.*)

Thoth had provided him he was able to paralyse all Āapep's limbs and to rise upon this world. Since then the "great gods," even though benevolently disposed towards them, were not able to deliver the dead from the devils that lived upon the "bodies, souls, spirits, shadows and hearts of the dead," the Egyptians decided to invoke the aid of Thoth on behalf of their dead and to place them under the protection of his almighty spells. Inspired by Thoth the theologians of ancient Egypt composed a large number of funerary texts which were certainly in general use under the IVth dynasty (about 3700 B.C.), and were probably well known under the Ist dynasty, and throughout the whole period of dynastic history Thoth was regarded as the author of the "Book of the Dead."

III.

THE BOOK PER-T EM HRU, OR [THE CHAPTERS OF] COMING
FORTH BY (OR, INTO) THE DAY, COMMONLY CALLED
THE "BOOK OF THE DEAD."

The spells and other texts which were written by Thoth for
the benefit of the dead, and are directly connected with him,
were called, according to documents written under the XIth
and XVIIIth dynasties, "Chapters of the Coming Forth by
(or, into) the Day," ⟨hieroglyphs⟩. One rubric
in the Papyrus of Nu (Brit. Mus. No. 10477) states that the text
of the work called "PER-T EM HRU," *i.e.*, "Coming Forth (or,
into) the Day," was discovered by a high official in the founda-
tions of a shrine of the god Ḥennu during the reign of Semti,
or Ḥesepti, a king of the Ist dynasty. Another rubric in the
same papyrus says that the text was cut upon the alabaster
plinth of a statue of Menkaurā (Mycerinus), a king of the
IVth dynasty, and that the letters were inlaid with lapis lazuli.
The plinth was found by Prince Ḥerutataf, ⟨hieroglyphs⟩, a
son of King Khufu (Cheops), who carried it off to his king and
exhibited it as a "most wonderful" thing. This composition
was greatly reverenced, for it "would make a man victorious
"upon earth and in the Other World ; it would ensure him a
"safe and free passage through the Ṭuat (Under World) ; it
"would allow him to go in and to go out, and to take at any
"time any form he pleased ; it would make his soul to flourish,
"and would prevent him from dying the [second] death." For
the deceased to receive the full benefit of this text it had to be
recited by a man "who was ceremonially pure, and who had
not eaten fish or meat, and had not consorted with women."
On coffins of the XIth dynasty and on papyri of the XVIIIth
dynasty we find two versions of the PER-T EM HRU, one long
and one short. As the title of the shorter version states that
it is the "Chapters of the PER-T EM HRU in a single chapter," it
is clear that this work, even under the IVth dynasty, contained
many "Chapters," and that a much abbreviated form of the
work was also current at the same period. The rubric that
attributes the "finding" of the Chapter to Ḥerutataf associates

it with Khemenu, *i.e.*, Hermopolis, and indicates that Thoth, the god of this city, was its author.

The work PER-T EM HRU received many additions in the

Scenes and texts from the Sixth Section of the Book of him that is in the Other World. From the sarcophagus of King Nekht-Heru-hebt, B.C. 378. [Southern Egyptian Gallery, Bay 25, No. 923.]

course of centuries, and at length, under the XVIIIth dynasty, it contained about 190 distinct compositions, or "Chapters." The original forms of many of these are to be found in the

"Pyramid Texts" (*i.e.*, the funerary compositions cut on the walls of the chambers and corridors of the pyramids of Kings Unās, Tetā, Pepi I Meri-Rā, Merenrā and Pepi II at Ṣaḳḳârah), which were written under the Vth and VIth dynasties. The forms which many other chapters had under the XIth and XIIth dynasties are well represented by the texts painted on the coffins of Amamu, Sen, and Guatep in the British Museum (Nos. 6654, 30839, 30841), but it is possible that both these and the so-called "Pyramid Texts" all belonged to the work PER-T EM HRU, and are extracts from it. The "Pyramid Texts" have no illustrations, but a few of the texts on the coffins of the XIth and XIIth dynasties have coloured vignettes, *e.g.*, those which refer to the region to be traversed by the deceased on his way to the Other World, and the Islands of the Blessed or the Elysian Fields. On the upper margins of the insides of such coffins there are frequently given two or more rows of coloured drawings of the offerings which under the Vth dynasty were presented to the deceased or his statue during the celebration of the service of "Opening the Mouth" and the performance of the ceremonies of "The Liturgy of Funerary Offerings." Under the XVIIIth dynasty, when the use of large rectangular coffins and sarcophagi fell somewhat into disuse, the scribes began to write collections of Chapters from the PER-T EM HRU on rolls of papyri instead of on coffins. At first the texts were written in hieroglyphs, the greater number of them being in black ink, and an attempt was made to illustrate each text by a vignette drawn in black outline. The finest known example of such a codex is the Papyrus of Nebseni (Brit. Mus. No. 9900), which is 77 feet 7½ inches in length and 1 foot 1½ inches in breadth. Early in the XVIIIth dynasty scribes began to write the titles of the Chapters, the rubrics, and the catchwords in red ink and the text in black, and it became customary to decorate the vignettes with colours, and to increase their size and number. The oldest codex of this class is the Papyrus of Nu (Brit. Mus. No. 10477) which is 65 feet 3½ inches in length, and 1 foot 1½ inches in breadth. This and many other rolls were written by their owners for their own tombs, and in each roll both text and vignettes were usually the work of the same hand. Later, however, the scribe wrote the text only, and a skilled artist was employed to add the coloured vignettes, for which spaces were marked out and left blank by the scribe. The finest example of this class of roll is the Papyrus of Ani

Vignette and text of the Theban Book of the Dead from the Papyrus of Nu. [Brit. Mus., No. 10477.] XVIIIth dynasty

Vignette and text of the Theban Book of the Dead from the Papyrus of Ani. [Brit. Mus., No. 10470.] XVIIIth dynasty.

(Brit. Mus., No. 10470), which is 78 feet in length and 1 foot 3 inches in breadth. In all papyri of this class the text is written in hieroglyphs, but under the XIXth and following dynasties many papyii are written throughout in the hieratic character ; these usually lack vignettes, but have coloured frontispieces.

Under the rule of the High Priests of Åmen many changes were introduced into the contents of the papyri, and the arrangement of the texts and vignettes of the PER-T EM HRU was altered. The great confraternity of Åmen-Rā, the " King of the Gods," felt it to be necessary to emphasize the supremacy of their god even in the Kingdom of Osiris, and they added many prayers, litanies and hymns to the Sun-god to every selection of the texts from the PER-T EM HRU that was copied on a roll of papyrus for funerary purposes. The greater number of the rolls of this period are short and contain only a few Chapters, e.g., the Papyrus of the Royal Mother Netchemet (Brit. Mus. No. 10541) and the Papyrus of Queen Netchemet (Brit. Mus. No. 10478). In some the text is very defective and carelessly written, but the coloured vignettes are remarkable for their size and beauty ; of this class of roll the finest example is the Papyrus of Ånhai (Brit. Mus. No. 10472). The most interesting of all the rolls that were written during the rule of the Priest-Kings over Upper Egypt is the Papyrus of Princess Nesitanebtashru (Brit. Mus. No. 10554), now commonly known as the " Greenfield Papyrus."

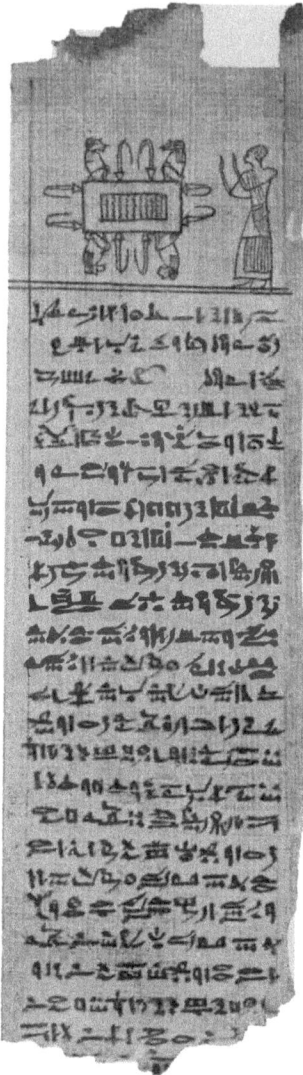

Vignette and Chapter of the Book of the Dead written in hieratic for Heru-em-heb.
[Brit. Mus., No. 10257.]
XXVIth dynasty, or later.

Her-Heru, the first priest-king, and Queen Netchemet standing in the Hall of Osiris and praying to the god whilst the heart of the Queen is being weighed in the Balance. XXIst dynasty, about B.C. 1050.

[Southern Egyptian Gallery, No. 758.] Presented by His Majesty the King, 1903.

It is the longest and widest funerary papyrus[1] known, for it measures 123 feet by 1 foot 6¼ inches, and it contains more Chapters, Hymns, Litanies, Adorations and Homages to the gods than any other roll. The 87 Chapters from the PER-T EM HRU which it contains prove the princess's devotion to the cult of Osiris, and the Hymns to Åmen-Rā show that she was able to regard this god and Osiris not as rivals but as two aspects of the same god. She believed that the "hidden" creative power which was materialized in Åmen was only another form of the power of procreation, renewed birth and resurrection which was typified by Osiris. The oldest copies of the PER-T EM HRU which we have on papyrus contain a few extracts from other ancient funerary works, such as the "Book of Opening the Mouth," the "Liturgy of Funerary Offerings," and the "Book of the Two Ways." But under the rule of the Priest-Kings the scribes incorporated with the Chapters of the PER-T EM HRU extracts from the "Book of Ami-Tuat" and the "Book of Gates," and several of the vignettes and texts that are found on the walls of the royal tombs of Thebes.

One of the most remarkable texts written at this period is found in the Papyrus of Nesi-Khensu, which is now in the Egyptian Museum in Cairo. This is really the copy of a contract which is declared to have been made between Nesi-Khensu and Åmen-Rā, "the holy god, the lord of all the gods." As a reward for the great piety of the queen, and her devotion to the interests of Åmen-Rā upon earth, the god undertakes to make her a goddess in his kingdom, to provide her with an estate there in perpetuity and a never-failing supply of offerings, and happiness of heart, soul and body, and the [daily] recital upon earth of the "Seventy Songs of Rā" for the benefit of her soul in the Khert-Neter, or Under World. The contract was drawn up in a series of paragraphs in legal phraseology by the priests of Åmen, who believed they had the power of making their god do as they pleased when they pleased.

Little is known of the history of the PER-T EM HRU after the downfall of the priests of Åmen, and during the period of the rule of the Nubians, but under the kings of the XXVIth dynasty

---

[1] The longest papyrus in the world is Papyrus Harris No. 1 (Brit. Mus. No. 9999) ; it measures 133 feet by 1 foot 4¼ inches.

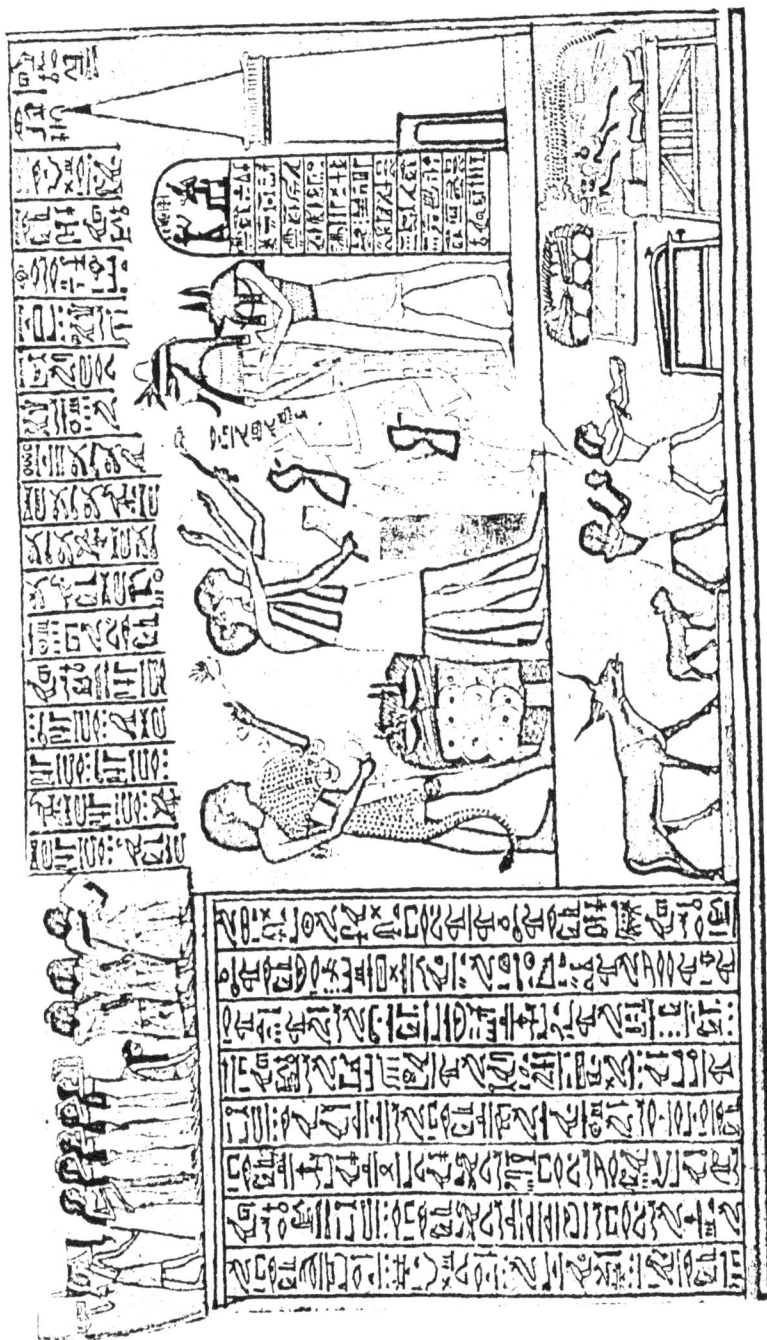

The Ceremony of "Opening of the Mouth" being performed on the mummy of the royal scribe Hunefer at the door of the tomb. [From Brit. Mus., Pap. No. 9901.]

the Book enjoyed a great vogue. Many funerary rolls were written both in hieroglyphs and hieratic, and were decorated with vignettes drawn in black outline ; and about this time the

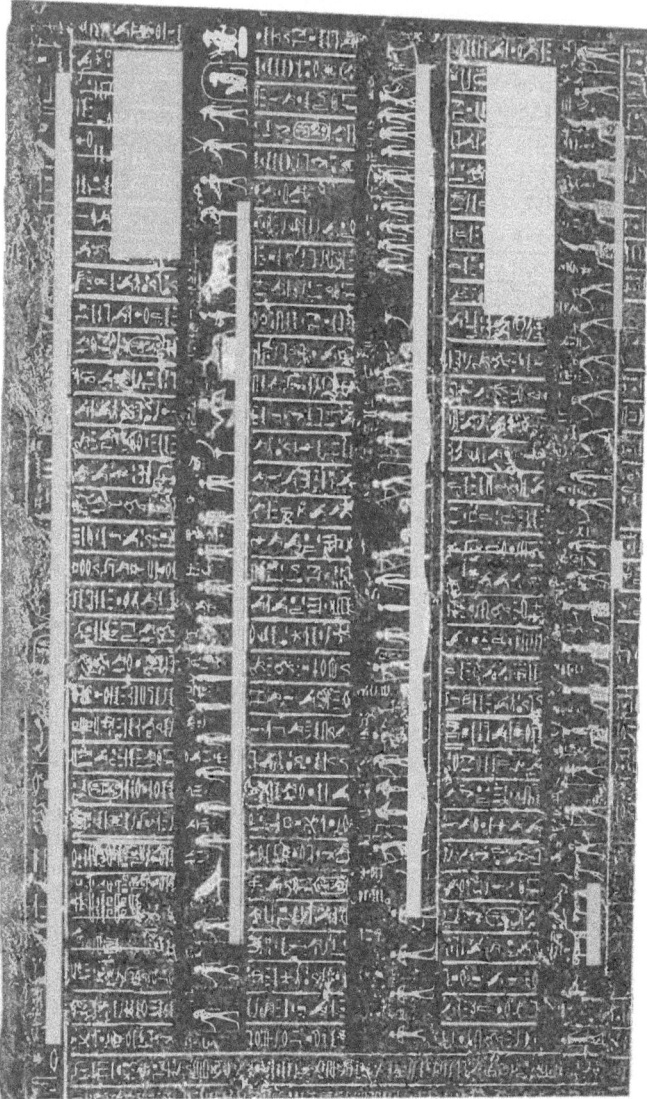

The journey of the Sun-god through the Third Section of the Other World.   From the sarcophagus of Nekht-Heru-hebt, king of Egypt, B.C. 378.
[Bay 25, No. 923.]

scribes began to write funerary texts in the demotic character. But men no longer copied long selections from the PER-T EM HRU as they had done under the XVIIIth, XIXth and XXth dynasties, partly because the religious views of the Egyptians had undergone a great change, and partly because a number of Books of the Dead of a more popular character had appeared. The cult of Osiris was triumphant everywhere, and men preferred the hymns and litanies which dealt with his sufferings, death and resurrection to the compositions in which the absolute supremacy of Rā and his solar cycle of gods and goddesses was assumed or proclaimed. Thus, in the " Lamentations of Isis " and the "Festival Songs of Isis and Nephthys," and the " Litanies of Seker," and the " Book of Honouring Osiris," etc., the central figure is Osiris, and he alone is regarded as the giver of everlasting life. The dead were no longer buried with large rolls of papyrus filled with Chapters of the PER-T EM HRU laid in their coffins, but with small sheets or strips of papyrus, on which were inscribed the above compositions, or the shorter texts of the " Book of Breathings," or the " Book of Traversing Eternity," or the" Book of May my name flourish," or a part of the " Chapter of the Last Judgment."

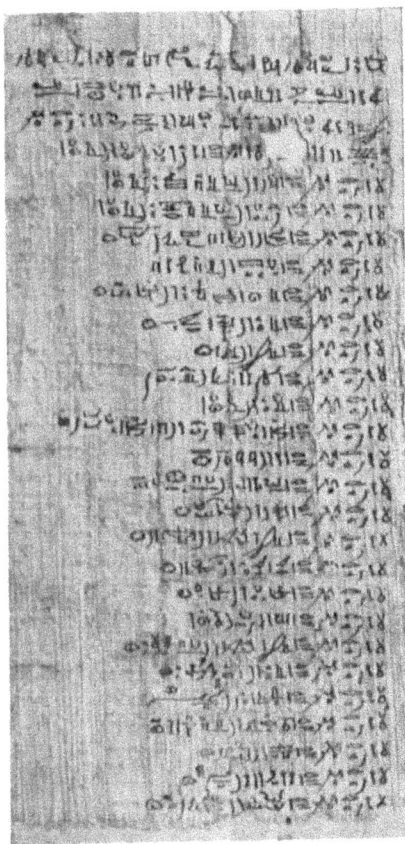

A copy of a Book of the Dead entitled " May my name flourish !"
[Brit. Mus., No. 10,304.]   Roman Period.

Ancient Egyptian tradition asserts that the Book PER-T EM HRU was used early in the Ist dynasty, and the papyri and coffins of the Roman Period afford evidence that the native

Egyptians still accepted all the essential beliefs and doctrines contained in it. During the four thousand years of its existence many additions were made to it, but nothing of importance seems to have been taken away from it. In the space here available it is impossible to describe in detail the various Recensions of this work, viz., (1) the Heliopolitan, (2) the Theban and its various forms, and (3) the Saïte ; but it is proposed to sketch briefly the main facts of the Egyptian Religion which may be deduced from them generally, and especially from the Theban Recension, and to indicate the contents of the principal Chapters. ˙ No one papyrus can be cited as a final authority, for no payprus contains all the Chapters, 190 in number, of the Theban Recension, and in no two papyri are the selection and sequence of the Chapters identical, or is the treatment of the vignettes the same.

IV.

Thoth, the Author of the Book of the Dead.

Thoth, in Egyptian Tchehuti or Ṭehuti, 𓅝𓏏𓎛𓏤𓀭 or 𓏏𓎛𓏤𓀭, who has already been mentioned as the author of the texts that form the PER-T EM HRU, or Book of the Dead, was believed by the Egyptians to have been the heart and mind of the Creator, who was in very early times in Egypt called by the natives "Pantti," and by foreigners "Rā." Thoth was also the "tongue " of the Creator, and he at all times voiced the will of the great god, and spoke the words which commanded every being and thing in heaven and in earth to come into existence. His words were almighty and once uttered never remained without effect. He framed the laws by which heaven, earth and all the heavenly bodies are maintained; he ordered the courses of the sun, moon, and stars; he invented drawing and design and the arts, the letters of the alphabet and the art of writing, and the science of mathematics. At a very

Teḥuti (Thoth).

early period he was called the " scribe (or secretary) of the Great Company of the Gods," and as he kept the celestial register of the words and deeds of men, he was regarded by many generations of Egyptians as the "Recording Angel." He was the inventor of physical and moral Law and became the personification of JUSTICE ; and as the Companies of the Gods of Heaven, and Earth, and the Other World appointed him to " weigh the words and deeds " of men, and his verdicts were unalterable, he became more powerful in the Other World than Osiris himself. Osiris owed his triumph over Set in the Great Judgment Hall of the Gods entirely to the skill of Thoth of the " wise mouth " as an Advocate, and to his influence with the gods in heaven. And every follower of Osiris relied

Set, the Arch-Liar and god of Evil.

upon the advocacy of Thoth to secure his acquittal on the Day of Judgment, and to procure for him an everlasting habitation in the Kingdom of Osiris.

V.

THOTH AND OSIRIS.

The Egyptians were not satisfied with the mere possession of the texts of Thoth, when their souls were being weighed in the Great Scales in the Judgment Hall of Osiris, but they also wished Thoth to act as their Advocate on this dread occasion and to prove their innocence as he had proved that of Osiris before the great gods in prehistoric times. According to a very ancient Egyptian tradition, the god Osiris, who was originally the god of the principle of the fertility of the Nile, became incarnate on earth as the son of Geb, the Earth-god, and Nut, the Sky-goddess. He had two sisters, Isis and Nephthys, and one brother, Set ; he married Isis and Set married Nephthys Geb set Osiris on the throne of Egypt, and his rule was beneficent and the nation was happy and prosperous. Set marked this and became very jealous of his brother, and wished to slay him so that he might seize his throne and take possession of Isis, whose reputation as a devoted and loving wife and able manager filled the country. By some means or other Set did contrive to kill Osiris : according to one story he killed him by the side of a canal at Neṭat, ⌇⌇⌇⌇, near Abydos, and according to another he caused him to be drowned. Isis, accompanied by her sister Nephthys, went to Neṭat and rescued the body of her lord, and the two sisters, with the help of Ånpu, a son of Rā the Sun-god, embalmed it. They then laid the body in a tomb, and a sycamore tree grew round it and flourished over the grave. A tradition which is found in the Pyramid Texts states that before Osiris was laid in his tomb, his wife Isis,

by means of her magical powers, succeeded in restoring him to life temporarily, and made him beget of her an heir, who was called Horus. After the burial of Osiris, Isis retreated to the marshes in the Delta, and there she brought forth Horus. In order to avoid the persecution of Set, who on one occasion succeeded in killing Horus by the sting of a scorpion, she fled from place to place in the Delta, and lived a very unhappy life for some years. But Thoth helped her in all her difficulties and provided her with the words of power which restored Horus to life, and enabled her to pass unharmed among the crocodiles and other evil beasts that infested the waters of the

Horus of Edfu spearing the Crocodile (?) Set.

Delta at that time.

When Horus arrived at years of maturity, he set out to find Set and to wage war against his father's murderer. At length they met and a fierce fight ensued, and though Set was defeated before he was finally hurled to the ground, he succeeded in tearing out the right eye of Horus and keeping it. Even after this fight Set was able to persecute Isis, and Horus was powerless to prevent it until Thoth made Set give him the right eye of Horus which he had carried off. Thoth then brought the eye to Horus, and replaced it in his face, and restored sight to it by spitting upon it. Horus then sought out the body of Osiris in order to raise it up to life, and when he found it he untied the bandages so that Osiris might move his limbs, and rise up. Under the direction of Thoth Horus recited a series of formulas as he presented offerings to Osiris, and

THE FOUR SONS OF HORUS.

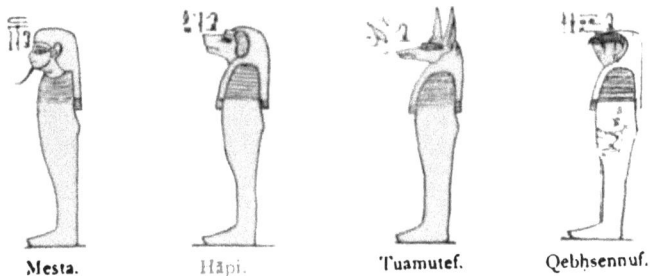

Mesta.　　Hapi.　　Tuamutef.　　Qebhsennuf.

he and his sons and Anubis performed the ceremonies which opened the mouth, and nostrils, and the eyes and the ears of

Anubis standing by the bier of the dead.

Osiris. He embraced Osiris and so transferred to him his *ka*, *i.e.*, his own living personality and virility, and gave him his eye which Thoth had rescued from Set and had replaced in his face. As soon as Osiris had eaten the eye of Horus he became endowed with a soul and vital power, and recovered thereby the complete use of all his mental faculties, which death had suspended. Straightway he rose up from his bier and became the Lord of the Dead and King of the Under World. Osiris became the type and symbol of resurrection among the Egyptians of all periods, because he was a god who had been originally a mortal and had risen from the dead.

But before Osiris became King of the Under World he suffered further persecution from Set. Piecing together a number of disconnected hints and brief statements in the texts, it seems pretty clear either that Osiris appealed to the " Great Gods " to take notice that Set had murdered him, or that Set brought a series of charges against Osiris. At all events the " Great Gods " determined to investigate the matter. The Greater and the Lesser Companies of the Gods assembled in the celestial Ȧnu, or Heliopolis, and ordered Osiris to stand up and defend himself against the charges brought against him by Set. Isis and Nephthys brought him before the gods, and Horus, " the avenger of his father," came to watch the case on behalf of his father, Osiris. Thoth appeared in the Hall of Judgment in his official capacity as " scribe," *i.e.*, secretary to the gods, and the hearing of the evidence began. Set seems to have pleaded his own cause, and to have repeated the charges which he had made against Osiris. The defence of Osiris was undertaken by Thoth, who proved to the gods that the charges brought against Osiris by Set were unfounded, that the statements of Set were lies, and that therefore Set was a liar. The gods accepted Thoth's proof of the innocence of Osiris and the guilt of Set, and ordered that Osiris was to be considered a Great God and to have rule over the Kingdom of the Under World, and that Set was to be punished. Thoth convinced them that Osiris was " MAȦ KHERU," " true of word," *i.e.*, that he had spoken the truth when he gave his evidence, and in texts of all periods Thoth is frequently described as S-MAȦ KHERU ȦSÀR,

𓀀 ... , *i.e.*, he who proved Osiris to be " true
of word." As for Set the Liar, he was seized by the ministers
of the Great Gods, who threw him down on his hands and face
and made Osiris mount upon his back as a mark of his victory
and superiority. After this Set was bound with cords like a
beast for sacrifice, and in the presence of Thoth was hacked in
pieces.

VI.

OSIRIS AS JUDGE OF THE DEAD AND KING OF THE UNDER WORLD.

When Set was destroyed Osiris departed from this world to
the kingdom which the gods had given him and began to reign
over the dead. He was absolute king of this realm, just as Rā
the Sun-god was absolute king of the sky. This region of the
dead, or Dead-land, is called " Ṭat," ... , or " Ṭuat,"
★ ... , but where the Egyptians thought it was situated
is not quite clear. The original home of the cult of Osiris was
in the Delta, in a city which in historic times was called Ṭetu by
the Egyptians and Busiris by the Greeks, and it is reasonable
to assume that the Ṭuat, over which Osiris ruled, was situated
near this place. Wherever it was it was not underground, and
it was not originally in the sky or even on its confines ; but it
was located on the borders of the visible world, in the Outer
Darkness. The Ṭuat was not a place of happiness, judging from
the description of it in the PER-T EM ḤRU, or Book of the Dead.
When Ani the scribe arrived there he said, "What is this to which
" I have come ? There is neither water nor air here, its depth
" is unfathomable, it is as dark as the darkest night, and men
" wander about here helplessly. A man cannot live here and
" be satisfied, and he cannot gratify the cravings of affection "
(Chapter CLXXV). In the Ṭuat there was neither tree nor plant,
for it was the "land where nothing grew " ; and in primitive
times it was a region of destruction and death, a place where
the dead rotted and decayed, a place of abomination, and horror
and terror, and annihilation. But in very early times, certainly

in the Neolithic Period, the Egyptians believed in some kind of a future life, and they dimly conceived that the attainment of that life might possibly depend upon the manner of life which those who hoped to enjoy it led here. The Egyptians "hated death and loved life," and when the belief gained ground among them that Osiris, the God of the Dead, had himself risen from the dead, and had been acquitted by the gods of heaven after a searching trial, and had the power to "make men and women to be born again," and "to renew life" because of his truth and righteousness, they came to regard him as the Judge as well as the God of the Dead. As time went on, and moral and religious ideas developed among the Egyptians, it became certain to them that only those who had satisfied Osiris as to their truth-speaking and honest dealing upon earth could hope for admission into his kingdom.

When the power of Osiris became predominant in the Under World, and his fame as a just and righteous judge became well established among the natives of Lower and Upper Egypt, it was universally believed that after death all men would appear before him in his dread Hall of Judgment to receive their reward or their sentence of doom. The writers of the Pyramid Texts, more than fifty-five centuries ago, dreamed of a time when heaven and earth and men did not exist, when the gods had not yet been born, when death had not been created,

, and when anger, speech (?), cursing and rebellion were unknown.[1] But that time was very remote, and long before the great fight took place between Horus and Set, when the former lost his eye and the latter was wounded in a vital part of his body. Meanwhile death had come into the world, and since the religion of Osiris gave man a hope of escape from death, and the promise of ever-lasting life of the peculiar kind that appealed to the great mass of the Egyptian people, the spread of the cult of Osiris and its ultimate triumph over all forms of religion in Egypt were assured. Under the early dynasties the priesthood of Ànu (the On of

---

[1] Pyramid of Pepi I, ll. 664 and 662.

the Bible) strove to make their Sun-god Rā pre-eminent in Egypt, but the cult of this god never appealed to the people as a whole. It was embraced by the Pharaohs, and their high officials, and some of the nobles, and the official priesthood, but the reward which its doctrine offered was not popular with the materialistic Egyptians. A life passed in the Boat of Rā with the gods, being arrayed in light and fed upon light, made no appeal to the ordinary folk since Osiris offered them as a reward a life in the Field of Reeds, and the Field of Offerings of Food, and the Field of the Grasshoppers, and everlasting existence in a transmuted and beatified body among the resurrected bodies of father and mother, wife and children, kinsfolk and friends.

But, as according to the cult of Rā, the wicked, the rebels, and the blasphemers of the Sun-god suffered swift and final punishment, so also all those who had sinned against the stern moral Law of Osiris, and who had failed to satisfy its demands, paid the penalty without delay. The Judgment of Rā was held at sunrise, and the wicked were thrown into deep pits filled with fire, and their bodies, souls, shadows and hearts were consumed forthwith. The Judgment of Osiris took place near Abydos, probably at midnight, and a decree of swift annihilation was passed by him on the damned. Their heads were cut off by the headsman of Osiris, who was called Shesmu, and their bodies dismembered and destroyed in pits of fire. There was no eternal punishment for men, for the wicked were annihilated quickly and completely ; but inasmuch as Osiris sat in judgment and doomed the wicked to destruction daily, the infliction of punishment never ceased.

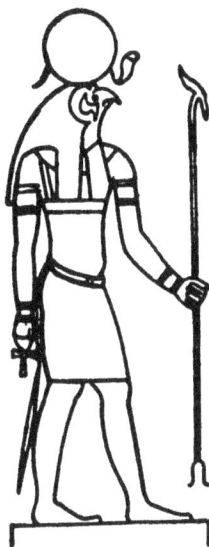

Rā the Sun-god.

VII.

THE JUDGMENT OF OSIRIS.

The oldest religious texts suggest that the Egyptians always associated the Last Judgment with the weighing of the heart in a pair of scales, and in the illustrated papyri of the Book of the Dead great prominence is always given to the vignettes in which this weighing is being carried out. The heart, *ab* ♡, was taken as the symbol of all the emotions, desires, and passions, both good and evil, and out of it proceeded the issues of life. It was intimately connected with the *ka*, ⊔, *i.e.*, the double or personality of a man, and several short spells in the Book PER-T EM HRU were composed to ensure its preservation (Chapters XXVI–XXXB). The great Chapter of the Judgment of Osiris, the CXXVth, is divided into three parts, which are sometimes (as in the Papyrus of Ani) prefaced by a Hymn to Osiris. The first part contains the following, which was said by the deceased when he entered the Hall of Maāti, in which Osiris sat in judgment:

" Homage to thee, O Great God, Lord of Maāti,[1] I have come
" to thee, O my Lord, that I may behold thy beneficence. I
" know thee, and I know thy name, and the names of the Forty-
" Two who live with thee in the Hall of Maāti, who keep ward
" over sinners, and feed upon their blood on the day of estimating
" characters before Un-Nefer[2] . . . Behold, I have come to
" thee, and I have brought *maāt* (*i.e.*, truth, integrity) to thee.
" I have destroyed sin for thee. I have not sinned against men.
" I have not oppressed [my] kinsfolk. I have done no wrong in
" the place of truth. I have not known worthless folk. I have
" not wrought evil. I have not defrauded the oppressed one
" of his, goods. I have not done the things that the gods
" abominate. I have not vilified a servant to his master. I
" have not caused pain. I have not let any man hunger. I
" have made no one to weep. I have not committed murder.
" I have not commanded any to commit murder for me. I have
" inflicted pain on no man. I have not defrauded the temples

---

[1] *I.e.*, Truth, or Law, in a double aspect.
[2] **A** name of Osiris.

"of their oblations. I have not purloined the cakes of the
"gods. I have not stolen the offerings to the spirits (*i.e.*, the
"dead). I have not committed fornication. I have not pol-
"luted myself in the holy places of the god of my city. I have
"not diminished from the bushel. I did not take from or add
"to the acre-measure. I did not encroach on the fields [of
"others]. I have not added to the weights of the scales. I
"have not misread the pointer of the scales. I have not taken
"milk from the mouths of children. I have not driven cattle
"from their pastures. I have not snared the birds of the gods.
"I have not caught fish with fish of their kind. I have not
"stopped water [when it should flow]. I have not cut the dam
"of a canal. I have not extinguished a fire when it should burn.
"I have not altered the times of the chosen meat offerings. I
"have not turned away the cattle [intended for] offerings. I
"have not repulsed the god at his appearances. I am pure.
"I am pure. I am pure. I am pure. . . ."

In the second part of Chapter CXXV Osiris is seen seated at
one end of the Hall of Maāti accompanied by the two goddesses
of Law and Truth, and the Forty-Two gods who are there to
assist him. Each of the Forty-Two gods represents one of the
nomes of Egypt and has a symbolic name. When the deceased
had repeated the magical names of the doors of the Hall, he
entered it and saw these gods arranged in two rows, twenty-one
on each side of the Hall. At the end, near Osiris, were the
Great Scales, under the charge of Ånpu (Anubis), and the
monster Āmemit, the Eater of the Dead, *i.e.*, of the hearts of
the wicked who were condemned in the Judgment of Osiris.
The deceased advanced along the Hall and, addressing each of the
Forty-Two gods by his name, declared that he had not committed a certain sin, thus :

"O Usekh-nemmit, comer forth from Ånu, I have not committed
        sin.
"O Fenti, comer forth from Khemenu, I have not robbed.
"O Neha-hāu, comer forth from Re-stau, I have not killed men.
"O Nebā, comer forth in retreating, I have not plundered the
        property of God.
"O Set-qesu, comer forth from Hensu, I have not lied.
"O Uammti, comer forth from Khebt, I have not defiled any
        man's wife.

"O Maa-ânuf, comer forth from Per-Menu, I have not defiled myself.

"O Tem-Sep, comer forth from Ṭeṭu, I have not cursed the king.

"O Nefer-Tem, comer forth from Ḥet-ka-Ptaḥ, I have not acted deceitfully ; I have not committed wickedness.

"O Nekhen, comer forth from Ḥeqāṭ, I have not turned a deaf ear to the words of the Law (or Truth)."

The names of most of the Forty-Two gods are not ancient but were invented by the priests probably about the same time as the names in the Book of Him that is in the Ṭuat and the Book of Gates, *i.e.*, between the XIIth and the XVIIIth dynasties. Their artificial character is shown by their meanings. Thus Usekh-nemmit means " He of the long strides " ; Fenṭi means " He of the Nose " ; Neḥa-ḥāu means " Stinking-members " ; Seṭ-qesu means " Breaker of bones," etc. The early Egyptologists called the second part of the CXXVth Chapter the "Negative Confession," and it is generally known by this somewhat inexact title to this day.

In the third part of the CXXVth Chapter comes the address which the deceased made to the gods after he had declared his innocence of the sins enumerated before the Forty-Two gods. He says : " Homage to you, O ye gods who dwell in your Hall " of Maāti. I know you and I know your names. Let me not " fall under your slaughtering knives. Bring not my wickedness " to the notice of the god whose followers ye are. Let not the " affair [of my judgment] come under your jurisdiction. Speak " ye the Law (or truth) concerning me before Neb-er-tcher,[1] " for I performed the Law (or, truth) in Ta-merā (*i.e.*, Egypt). " I have not blasphemed the God. No affair of mine came under " the notice of the king in his day. Homage to you, O ye who " are in your Hall of Maāti, who have no lies in your bodies, " who live on truth, who eat truth before Horus, the dweller " in his disk, deliver ye me from Babai[2] who liveth upon the " entrails of the mighty ones on the day of the Great Reckoning " (ÁPT ĀAT, 𓍯𓍯𓍯𓍯𓍯𓍯). Behold me ! I have come

---

[1] *I.e.*, the " Lord to the uttermost limit of everything," or God.

[2] 𓍯𓍯𓍯𓍯𓍯𓍯, he was according to one legend the firstborn son of Osiris.

" to you without sin, without deceit (?), without evil, without
" false testimony (?) I have not done an [evil] thing. I live upon
" truth and I feed upon truth. I have performed the behests
" of men, and the things that satisfy the gods.[1] I have pro-
" pitiated the God [by doing] His will. I have given bread to the
" hungry, water to the thirsty, raiment to the naked, and a boat
" to him that needed one. I have made holy offerings to the
" gods, and sepulchral offerings to the beatified dead. Be ye
" then my saviours, be ye my protectors, and make no accusa-
" tion against me before the Great God. I am pure of mouth,
" and clean of hands ; therefore it hath been said by those who
" saw me, ' Come in peace, come in peace.' "

The deceased then addresses Osiris, and says, " Hail, thou
" who art exalted upon thy standard, thou Lord of the Atefu
" Crown, whose name is ' Lord of Winds,' save me from thy
" Messengers (or Assessors) with uncovered faces, who bring
" charges of evil and make shortcomings plain, because I have
" performed the Law (or Truth) for the Lord of the Law (or
" Truth). I have purified myself with washings in water, my
" back hath been cleansed with salt, and my inner parts are in
" the Pool of Truth. There is not a member of mine that
" lacketh truth." From the lines that follow the above in the
Papyrus of Nu it seems as though the judgment of the deceased
by the Forty-Two gods was preliminary to the final judgment
of Osiris. At all events, after questioning him about the performance of certain ceremonies, they invited him to enter the
Hall of Maāti, but when he was about to do so the porter, and
the door-bolts, and the various parts of the door and its frame,
and the floor, refused to permit him to enter until he had repeated
their magical names. When he had pronounced these correctly
the porter took him in and presented him to Maau (?)-Taui, who
was Thoth himself. When asked by him why he had come the
deceased answered, " I have come that report may be made of
me." Then Thoth said, " What is thy condition ? " And
the deceased replied, " I am purified from evil things, I am free
" from the wickedness of those who lived in my days ; I am not
" one of them." On this Thoth said, " Thou shalt be reported.
" [Tell me :] Who is he whose roof is fire, whose walls are living

---

[1] *I.e.,* I have kept the Moral and Divine Law.

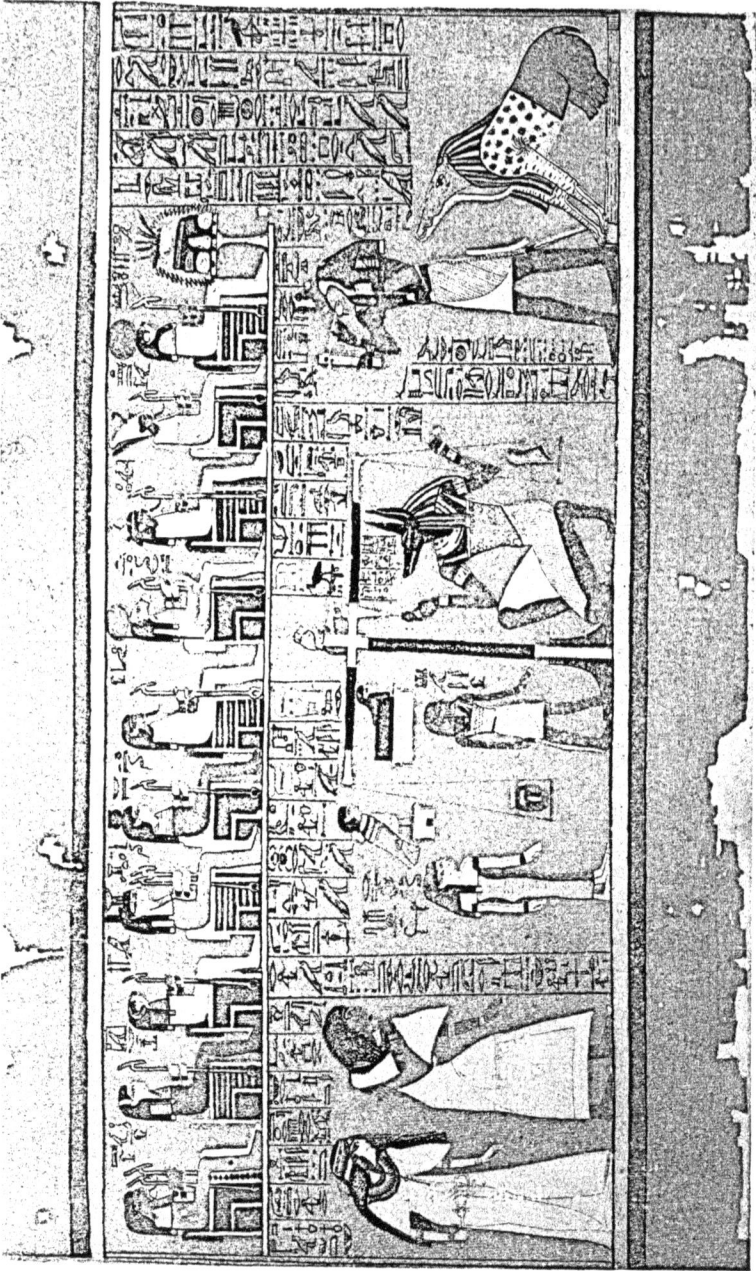

The wei... of the heart of the Scribe Ani in th

"serpents, and whose floor is a stream of water? Who is
"he?" The deceased having replied "Osiris," Thoth then
led him forward to the god Osiris, who received him, and promised that subsistence should be provided for him from the
Eye of Rā.

In great papyri of the Book of the Dead such as those of
Nebseni, Nu, Ani, Hunefer, etc., the Last Judgment, or the
"Great Reckoning," is made the most prominent scene in the
whole work, and the vignette in which it is depicted is several
feet long. The most complete form of it is given in the Papyrus
of Ani, and may be thus described : At one end of the Hall of
Maāti Osiris is seated on a throne within a shrine made in the
form of a funerary coffer ; behind him stand Isis and Nephthys.
Along one side of the Hall are seated the gods Harmachis,
Tem, Shu, Tefnut, Geb, Nut, Isis and Nephthys, Horus, Hathor,
Hu and Saa, who are to serve as the divine jury ; these formed
the "Great Company of the Gods" of Ànu (Heliopolis). By
these stands the Great Balance, and on its pillar sits the dog-
headed ape Àstes, or Àstenu, the associate of Thoth. The
pointer of the Balance is in the charge of Ànpu. Behind Ànpu
are Thoth the scribe of the gods, and the monster Āmemit, with
the head of a crocodile, the forepaws and shoulders of a lion,
and the hindquarters of a hippopotamus ; the duty of the last-
named was to eat up the hearts that were light in the balance.
On the other side of the Balance Ani, accompanied by his wife,
is seen standing with head bent low in adoration, and between
him and the Balance stand the two goddesses who nurse and
rear children, Meskhenet and Rennet, Ani's soul, in the form of
a man-headed hawk, a portion of his body, and his luck Shai.
Since the heart was considered to be the seat of all will, emotion,
feeling, reason and intelligence, Ani's heart, $\eth$, is seen in
one pan of the Balance, and in the other is the feather, $\int$,
symbolic of truth and righteousness. Whilst his heart was in
the Balance Ani, repeating the words of Chapter XXXB of the
Book of the Dead, addressed it, saying, "My heart of my
"mother! My heart of my mother! My heart of my being!
"Make no stand against me when testifying, thrust me not
"back before the Tchatchaut (i.e., the overseers of Osiris), and
"make no failure in respect of me before the Master of the

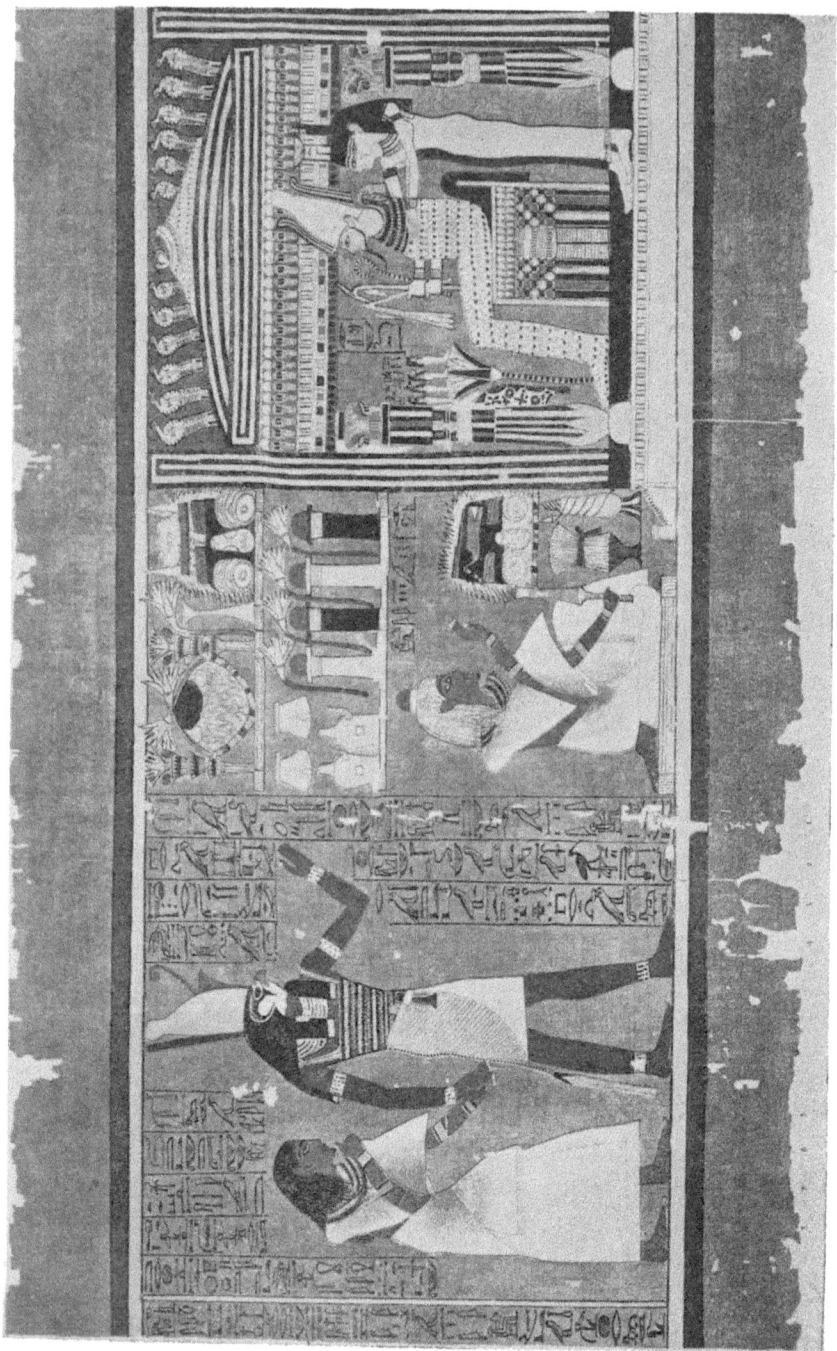

"Balance. Thou art my Ka, the dweller in my body, uniting (?)
"and strengthening my members. Thou shalt come forth to
"the happiness to which we advance. Make not my name to
"stink with the officers [of Osiris] who made men, utter no lie
"against me before the Great God, the Lord of Amentt."

Then Thoth, the Judge of Truth, of the Great Company of
the Gods who are in the presence of Osiris, saith to the gods,
"Hearken ye to this word : In very truth the heart of Osiris
"hath been weighed, and his soul hath borne testimony con-
"cerning him ; according to the Great Balance his case is
"truth (*i.e.*, just). No wickedness hath been found in him. He
"did not filch offerings from the temples. He did not act
"crookedly, and he did not vilify folk when he was on earth."

And the Great Company of the Gods say to Thoth, who
dwelleth in Khemenu (Hermopolis): "This that cometh
"forth from thy mouth of truth is confirmed (?) The Osiris,
"the scribe Ani, true of voice, hath testified. He hath not
"sinned and [his name] doth not stink before us ; Āmemit
"(*i.e.*, the Eater of the Dead) shall not have the mastery over
"him. Let there be given unto him offerings of food and an
"appearance before Osiris, and an abiding homestead in the
"Field of Offerings as unto the Followers of Horus."

Thus the gods have declared that Ani is "true of voice,"
as was Osiris, and they have called Ani "Osiris," because in his
purity of word and deed he resembled that god. In all the
copies of the Book of the Dead the deceased is always called
"Osiris," and as it was always assumed that those for whom
they were written would be found innocent when weighed in
the Great Balance, the words "true of voice," which were
equivalent in meaning to "innocent and acquitted," were always
written after their names. It may be noted in passing that
when Ani's heart was weighed against Truth, the beam of the
Great Balance remained perfectly horizontal. This suggests that
the gods did not expect the heart of the deceased to "kick the
beam," but were quite satisfied if it exactly counterbalanced
Truth. They demanded the fulfilment of the Law and nothing
more, and were content to bestow immortality upon the man
on whom Thoth's verdict was "he hath done no evil,"

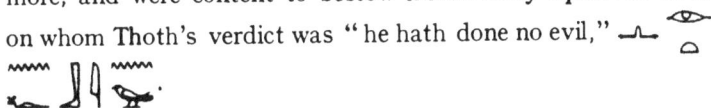

In accordance with the command of the gods Ani passes from the Great Balance to the end of the Hall of Maāti where Osiris is seated, and as he approaches the god Horus, the son of Isis, takes him by the hand and leads him forward, and standing before his father Osiris says, " I have come to thee, Un-Nefer,[1] " I have brought to thee the Osiris Ani. His heart is righteous " [and] hath come forth from the Balance. It hath no sin " before any god or any goddess. Thoth hath set down his " judgment in writing, and the Company of the Gods have " declared on his behalf that [his] evidence is very true. Let " there be given unto him of the bread and beer which appear " before Osiris. Let him be like the Followers of Horus for " ever ! " Next we see Ani kneeling in adoration before Osiris, and he says, " Behold, I am in thy presence, O Lord of Amentt. " There is no sin in my body. I have not uttered a lie know- " ingly. [I have] no duplicity (?) Grant that I may be like " the favoured (or rewarded) ones who are in thy train." Under favour of Osiris Ani then became a sā*ḥu*, ⎯⎯ 𓀀 𓆼 𓏏 𓃾, or " spirit-body," and in this form passed into the Kingdom of Osiris.

VIII.

THE KINGDOM OF OSIRIS.

According to the Book of Gates and the other " Guides " to the Egyptian Under World, the Kingdom of Osiris formed the Sixth Division of the Ṭuat ; in very early times it was situated in the Western Delta, but after the XIIth dynasty theologians placed it near Abydos in Upper Egypt, and before the close of the Dynastic Period the Ṭuat of Osiris had absorbed the Under World of every nome of Egypt. When the soul in its beatified or spirit body arrived there, the ministers of Osiris took it to the homestead or place of abode which had been allotted to it by the command of Osiris, and there it began its new existence. The large vignette to the CXth Chapter shows us exactly what manner of place the abode of the blessed was. The country was flat and the fields were intersected by canals

---

[1] *I.e.*, the " Beneficent Being," a title of Osiris.

of running water in which there were " no fish and no worms "
(*i.e.*, water snakes). In one part of it were several small
islands, and on one of them Osiris was supposed to dwell with
his saints. It was called the "·Island of Truth," and the ferry-
man of Osiris would not convey to it any soul that had not been
declared " true of word " by Thoth, Osiris and the Great Gods
at the " Great Reckoning." The portion of the Kingdom of
Osiris depicted in the large Books of the Dead represents in
many respects a typical Egyptian farm, and we see the deceased
engaged in ploughing and reaping and driving the oxen that
are treading out the corn. He was introduced into the Sekhet
Heteput (a section of the Sekhet Àaru, *i.e.*, " Field of Reeds,"
or the " Elysian Fields ") by Thoth, and there he found the souls
of his ancestors, who were joined to the Company of the Gods.
One corner of this region was specially set apart for the dwelling
place of the *àakhu*, *i.e.*, beatified souls, or spirit-souls, who were
said to be seven cubits in height, and to reap wheat or barley
which grew to a height of three cubits. Near this spot were
moored two boats that were always ready for the use of the
denizens of that region ; they appear to have been " spirit
boats," *i.e.*, boats which moved of themselves and carried the
beatified wheresoever they wanted to go without any trouble
or fatigue on their part.

How the beatified passed their time in the Kingdom of
Osiris may be seen from the pictures cut on the alabaster sarcophagus of Seti I, now preserved in Sir John Soane's Museum in
Lincoln's Inn Fields. Here we see them occupied in producing
the celestial food on which they and the god lived. Some are
tending the wheat plants as they grow, and others are reaping
the ripe grain. In the texts that accompany these scenes the
ears of wheat are said to be the " members of Osiris," and the
wheat plant is called the *maāt* plant. Osiris was the Wheat-god
and also the personification of *Maāt* (*i.e.*, Truth), and the
beatified· lived upon the body of their god and ate him daily,
and the substance of him was the " Bread of Everlastingness,"
which is mentioned .in the Pyramid Texts. The beatified are
described as " Those who have offered up incense to the gods,
" and whose *kau* (*i.e.*, doubles, or persons) have been washed
" clean. . They have been reckoned up and they are *maāt* (*i.e.*,
" Truth) in the presence of the Great God who destroyeth sin."

Osiris says to them, " Ye are truth of truth   rest in peace "
And of them he says " They were doers of truth whilst they were

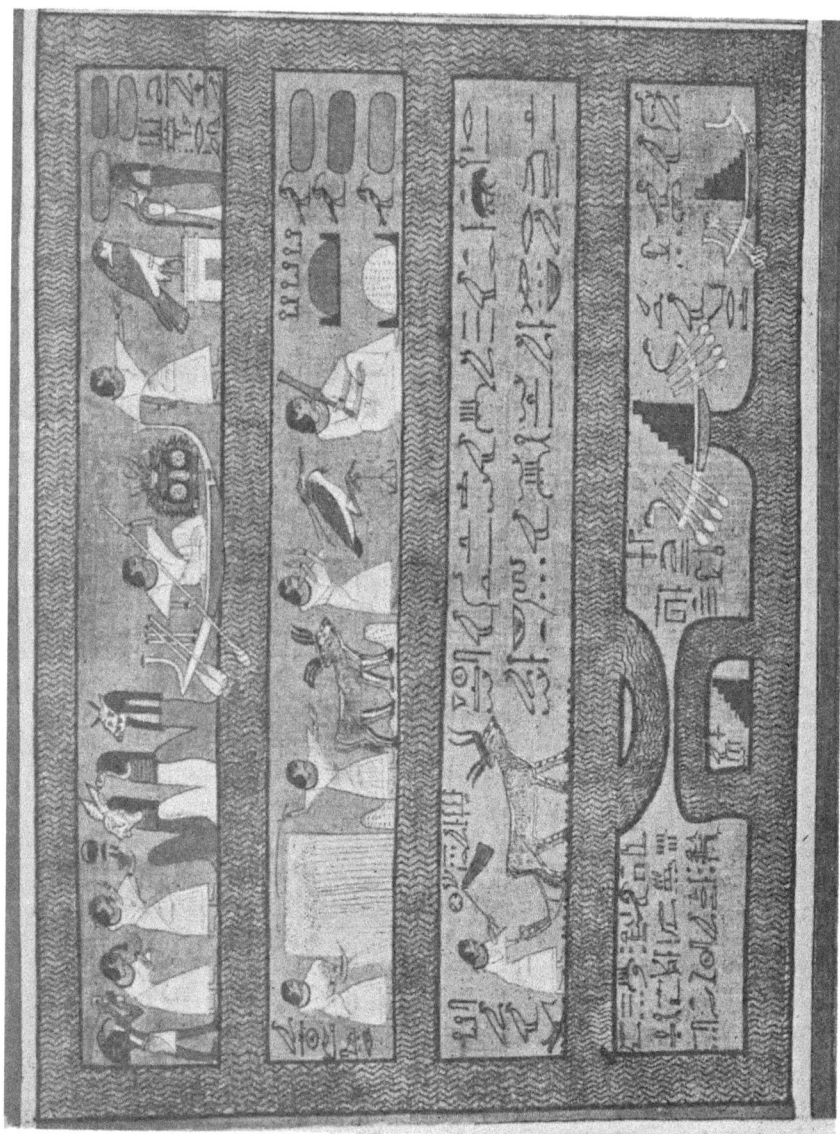

"upon earth, they did battle for their god and they shall be
" called to the enjoyment of the Land of the House of Life with

" Truth. Their truth shall be reckoned to them in the presence
" of the Great God who destroyeth sin." Then addressing them
again Osiris says, " Ye are beings of Truth, O ye Truths. Take
" ye your rest because of what ye have done, becoming even
" as those who are in my following, and who direct the House
" of Him whose Soul is holy. Ye shall live there even as they
" live, and ye shall have dominion over the cool waters of your
" land. I command that ye have your being to the limit [of
" that land] with Truth and without sin." In these passages
we have the two conceptions of Osiris well illustrated. As the
Wheat-god he would satisfy those who wished for a purely
material, agricultural heaven, where hunger would be unknown
and where the blessed would be able to satisfy every physical
desire and want daily ; and as the God of Truth, of whom the
spiritually minded hoped to become the counterpart, he would
be their hope, and consolation, and the image of the Eternal
God.

IX

A short description of the " Doors " or Chapters of the Book of the Dead.

All the great papyri of the Book of the Dead begin with a
Hymn to Rā, who from the period of the IVth dynasty was the
" King of the Gods " of Egypt. His cult was finally " established " under the Vth dynasty when the king of Egypt began
to call himself in official documents and monuments " Son of the
Sun," *Sa Rā.* This Hymn is supposed to be sung by
the deceased, who says :—

" Homage to thee, O Rā, at thy beauteous rising. Thou risest,
thou risest; thou shinest, thou shinest at the dawn. Thou art King
of the Gods, and the Maāti goddesses embrace thee. The Company of
the Gods praise thee at sunrise and at sunset. Thou sailest over the
heights of heaven and thy heart is glad. Thy Morning Boat meeteth
thy Evening Boat with fair winds. Thy father is the Sky-god and thy
mother is the Sky-goddess, and thou art Horus of the Eastern and
Western skies. . . . O thou Only One, O thou Perfect One, O
thou who art eternal, who art never weak, whom no mighty one can
abase; none hath dominion over the things which appertain to thee.
Homage to thee in thy characters of Horus, Tem, and Kheperā, thou
Great Hawk, who makest man to rejoice by thy beautiful face. When
thou risest men and women live. Thou renewest thy youth, and dost

set thyself in the place where thou wast yesterday. O Divine Youth, who art self-created, I cannot comprehend thee. Thou art the lord of heaven and earth, and didst create beings celestial and beings terrestrial. Thou art the God One, who camest into being in the beginning of time. Thou didst create the earth, and man, thou didst make the sky and the celestial river Hep; thou didst make the waters and didst give life unto all that therein is. Thou hast knit together the mountains, thou hast made mankind and the beasts of the field to come into being, and hast made the heavens and the earth. The fiend Nak is overthrown, his arms are cut off. O thou Divine Youth, thou heir of everlastingness, self-begotten and self-born, One, Might, of myriad forms and aspects, Prince of Ân (i.e., On), Lord of Eternity, Everlasting Ruler, the Company of the Gods rejoice in thee. As thou risest thou growest greater : thy rays are upon all faces. Thou art unknowable, and no tongue can describe thy similitude; thou existest alone. Millions of years have passed over the world, I cannot tell the number of those through which thou hast passed. Thou journeyest through spaces [requiring] millions of years [to pass over] in one little moment of time, and then thou settest and dost make an end of the hours."

The subject matter of the above extract is treated at greater length in Chapter XV, which contains a long Hymn to Râ at his rising, or Âmen-Râ, or Râ united to other solar gods, e.g., Horus and Kheperâ, and a short Hymn to Râ at his setting. In the latter the welcome which Râ receives from the dwellers in Âmentt (i.e., the Hidden Place, like the Greek " Hades ") is emphasized thus :—

"All the beatified dead (Âakhu) in the Tuat receive him in the horizon of Âmentt. They shout praises of him in his form of Tem (i.e., the setting sun). Thou didst rise and put on strength, and thou settest, a living being, and thy glories are in Âmentt. The gods of Âmentt rejoice in thy beauties (or beneficence). The hidden ones worship thee, the aged ones bring thee offerings and protect thee. The Souls of Âmentt cry out, and when they meet thy Majesty (Life, Strength, Health be to thee !) they shout ' Hail! Hail ! ' The lords of the mansions of the Tuat stretch out their hands to thee from their abodes, and they cry to thee, and they follow in thy bright train, and the hearts of the lords of the Tuat rejoice when thou sendest thy light into Âmentt. Their eyes follow thee, they press forward to see thee, and their hearts rejoice at the sight of thy face. Thou hearkenest to the petitions of those who are in their tombs, thou dispellest their helplessness and drivest away evil from them. Thou givest breath to their nostrils. Thou art greatly feared, thy form is majestic, and very greatly art thou beloved by those who dwell in the Other World."

The Introductory HYMN TO Rā is followed by a HYMN TO
OSIRIS, in which the deceased says :—

" Glory be to thee, O Osiris Un-Nefer, thou great god in Ábṭu
(Abydos), King of Eternity, Lord of Everlastingness, God whose
existence is millions of years, eldest son of Nut, begotten by Geb, the
Ancestor-Chief, Lord of the Crowns of the South and the North, Lord
of the High White Crown. Thou art the Governor of gods and of men
and hast received the sceptre, the whip, and the rank of thy Divine
Fathers. Let thy heart in Ámentt be content, for thy son Horus
is seated upon thy throne. Thou art Lord of Ṭeṭu (Busiris) and
Governor of Ábṭu (Abydos). Thou makest fertile the Two Lands (*i.e.*,
all Egypt) by [thy] true word before the Lord to the Uttermost Limit.
. . . Thy power is widespread, and great is the terror of thy name
' Osiris.' Thou endurest for all eternity in thy name of ' Un-Nefer '
(*i.e.*, Beneficent Being). Homage to thee, King of kings, Lord of
lords, Governor of governors, who from the womb of the Sky-goddess
hast ruled the World and the Under World. Thy limbs are as silver-
gold, thy hand is blue like lapis-lazuli, and the space on either side of
thee is of the colour of turquoise (or emerald). Thou god An of
millions of years, thy body is all-pervading, O dweller in the Land of
Holiness, thy face is beautiful. . . . The gods come before thee
bowing low. They hold thee in fear. They withdraw and retreat
when they see the awfulness of Rā upon thee ; the [thought] of the
conquests of thy Majesty is in their hearts. Life is with thee.
" Let me follow thy Majesty as when I was on earth, let my soul be
summoned, and let it be found near the Lords of Truth. I have come
to the City of God, the region that is eternally old, with my soul (*ba*),
double (*ka*) and spirit-soul (*ḍakhu*), to be a dweller in this land. Its
God is the Lord of Truth . . . he giveth old age to him that
worketh Truth, and honour to his followers, and at the last abundant
equipment for the tomb, and burial in the Land of Holiness. I have
come unto thee, my hands hold Truth, and there is no falsehood in my
heart. . . . Thou hast set Truth before thee ; I know on what
thou livest. I have committed no sin in this land, and I have defrauded
no man of his possessions." (Chapter CLXXXIII.)

Chapter I was recited by the priest who accompanied the
mummy to the tomb and performed the burial ceremonies
there. In it the priest (*kher ḥeb*) assumed the character of
Thoth and promised the deceased to do for him all that he had
done for Osiris in days of old. Chapter IB gave the *sāḥu*, or
" spirit-body," power to enter the Ṭuat immediately after the
burial of the material body, and delivered it from the Nine
Worms that lived on the dead. Chapters II–IV are short spells
written to give the deceased power to revisit the earth, to join the
gods, and to travel about the sky. Chapters V and VI provided

for the performance of agricultural labours in the Other World. The text of Chapter VI was cut on figures made of stone, wood, etc. (*ushabtiu*), which were placed in the tomb, and when the deceased recited it these figures became alive and did everything he wished. The *shabti* figure, 𓏠𓏠 𓅓 𓂝, took the place of the human funerary sacrifice which was common all over Egypt before the general adoption of the cult of Osiris under the XIIth dynasty. About 700 *ushabtiu* figures were found in the tomb of Seti I, and many of them are in the British Museum. Chapter VII is a spell to destroy the Great Serpent Āapep, 𓂋𓂋 𓈖𓈖 𓆙, the Arch-enemy of Horus the Elder, Rā, Osiris, Horus son of Isis, and of every follower of Osiris. Chapters VIII and IX secured a passage for the deceased through the Ţuat, and Chapters X and XI gave him power over the enemies he met there. Chapters XII and XIII gave him great freedom of movement in the Kingdom of Osiris. Chapter XIV is a prayer in which Osiris is entreated to put away any feeling of dissatisfaction that he may have for the deceased, who says, "Wash away my sins, Lord of Truth ; destroy my transgressions, "wickedness and iniquity, O God of Truth. May this god be at "peace with me. Destroy the things that are obstacles between "us. Give me peace, and remove all dissatisfaction from thy "heart in respect of me."

Chapter XV has several forms, and each of them contains Hymns to Rā, which were sung daily in the morning and

The holy Ape-gods singing hymns of praise to Rā at sunrise.

The Jackal-gods and the Hawk-gods singing hymns of praise to Rā at sunset.

evening; specimen paragraphs are given above (pp. 33, 34).
Chapter XVI is only a vignette that illustrates Chapter XV,
Chapter XVII is a very important chapter, for it contains state-
ments of divine doctrine as understood by the priests of Heliopolis.
The opening words are, " I am Tem in rising. I am the Only One.
" I came into being in Nu (the Sky). I am Rā, who rose in
" primeval time, ruler of what he had made." Following this
comes the question, " Who is this ? " and the answer is, " It is
" Rā who rose in the city of Ḥensu, in primeval time, crowned as

The Sun-god Rā, in the form of the " Great Cat," sitting by the side of the Persea
Tree of Anu, and cutting off the head of Āapep, the god of darkness and evil.

" king. He existed on the height of the Dweller in Khemenu
" (*i.e.*, Thoth of Hermopolis) before the pillars that support the
" sky were made." Chapter XVIII contains the Addresses to
Thoth, who is entreated to make the deceased to be declared
innocent before the gods of Heliopolis, Busiris, Latopolis, Mendes,
Abydos, etc. These addresses formed a very powerful spell
which was used by Horus, and when he recited it four times all
his enemies were overthrown and cut to pieces. Chapters XIX
and XX are variant forms of Chapter XVIII. Chapters XXI-
XXIII secured the help of Thoth in " opening the mouth " of
the deceased, whereby he obtained the power to breathe and
think and drink and eat. Thoth recited spells over the gods
whilst Ptaḥ untied the bandages and Shu forced open their
mouths with an iron (?) knife. Chapter XXIV gave to the
deceased a knowledge of the " words of power '" (𓎛𓏤𓅡𓊪 ,
ḥekau) which were used by the great god Tem-Kheperā, and
Chapter XXV restored to him his memory. Five chapters,
XXVI-XXX, contain prayers and spells whereby the deceased

obtained power over his heart and gained absolute possession of it. The most popular prayer is that of Chapter XXXB (see above, p. 4) which, according to its rubric, was "found," *i.e.*, edited, by Ḥerutataf, the son of the great Cheops, about 3600 B.C. This prayer was still in use in the early years of the Christian Era. In the Papyrus of Nu it is associated with Chapter LXIV, and the earliest form of it was probably in existence under the Ist dynasty.

Chapters XXXI–XLII were written to deliver the deceased from the Great Crocodile Sui, and the Serpents Rerek and Seksek, and the Lynx with its deadly claws, and the Beetle Āpshait, and the terrible Merti snake-goddesses, and a group of three particularly venomous serpents, and Āapep a personification of Set the god of evil, and the Eater of the Ass, and a series of beings who lived by slaughtering the souls of the dead. In Chapter XLII every member of the deceased is put under the protection of, or identified with, a god or goddess, *e.g.*, the hair with Nu, the face with Àten (*i.e.*, the solar disk), the eyes with Hathor, and the deceased exclaims triumphantly, "There is no member of my body which is not the member of a god." Chapter XLIII. A spell to prevent the decapitation of the deceased, who assumes in it the character of Osiris the Lord of Eternity. Chapter XLIV. An ancient and mighty spell, the recital of which prevented the deceased from dying a second time. Chapters XLV and XLVI preserved the mummy of the deceased from decay, and Chapter XLVII prevented the removal of his seat or throne. Chapter L enabled the deceased to avoid the block of execution of the god Shesmu. Chapters LI–LIII provided the deceased with pure food and clean water from the table of the gods; he lived upon what they lived upon, and so became one with them. Chapters LIV–LXII gave the deceased power to obtain cool water from the Celestial Nile and the springs of waters of heaven, and being identified with Shu, the god of light and air, he was enabled to pass over all the earth at will. His life was that of the Egg of the "Great Cackler," and the goddess Sesheta built a house for him in the Celestial Ànu, or Heliopolis.

The recital of Chapter LXIII enabled the deceased to avoid drinking boiling water in the Ṭuat. The water in some of its pools was cool and refreshing to those who were speakers of the truth, but it turned into boiling water and scalded the wicked when they tried to drink of it. Chapter LXIV is an epitome of the whole Book of the Dead, and it formed a " great and divine protection" for the deceased. The text is of a mystical character and suggests that the deceased could, through its recital, either absorb the gods into his being, or become himself absorbed by them. Its rubric orders abstention from meats, fish and women on the part of those who were to recite it. Chapter LXV gave the deceased victory over all his enemies, and Chapters LXVI and LXVII gave him access to the Boat of Rā. Chapters LXVIII–LXX procured him complete freedom of motion in heaven and on earth. Chapter LXXI is a series of addresses to the Seven Spirits who punished the wicked in the Kingdom of Osiris, and Chapter LXXII aided the deceased to be reborn in the Mesqet Chamber. The Mesqet was originally a bull's skin in which the deceased was wrapped. Chapter LXXIII is the same as Chapter IX. Chapters LXXIV and LXXV secured a passage for the deceased in the Henu Boat of Seker the Death-god, and Chapter LXXVI brought to his help the praying mantis which guided him through the "bush" to the House of Osiris. By the recital of Chapters LXXVII–LXXXVIII, i.e., the "Chapters of Transformations," the deceased was enabled to assume at will the forms of (1) the Golden Hawk, (2) the Divine Hawk, (3) the Great Self-created

The soul visiting the mummified body in the tomb. The bird-goddess at the head is Isis, and that at the feet is Nephthys.

God, (4) the Light-god or the Robe of Nu, (5) the Pure Lily, (6) the Son of Ptah, (7) the Benu Bird, (8) the Heron, (9) the Soul of Rā, (10) the Swallow, (11) the Sata or Earth-serpent, (12) the Crocodile. Chapter LXXXIX brought the soul (ba)

of the deceased to his body in the Ṭuat, and Chapter XC preserved him from mutilation and attacks of the god who "cut off heads and slit foreheads." Chapters XCI and XCII prevented the soul of the deceased from being shut in the tomb. Chapter XCIII is a spell very difficult to understand. Chapters XCIV and XCV provided the deceased with the books of Thoth and the power of this god, and enabled him to take his place as the scribe of Osiris. Chapters XCVI and XCVII also placed him under the protection of Thoth. The recital of Chapter XCVIII provided the deceased with a boat in which to sail over the northern heavens, and a ladder by which to ascend to heaven. Chapters XCIX–CIII gave him the use of the magical boat, the mystic name of each part of which he was obliged to know, and helped him to enter the Boat of Rā and to be with Hathor. The Bebait, or mantis, led him to the great gods (Chapter CIV), and the Uatch amulet from the neck of Rā provided his double (*ka*) and his heart-soul (*ba*) with offerings (Chapters CV, CVI). Chapters CVII–CIX made him favourably known to the spirits of the East and West, and the gods of the Mountain of Sunrise. In this region lived the terrible Serpent-god Ȧmi-hem-f ; he was 30 cubits (50 feet) long. In the East the deceased saw the Morning Star, and the Two Sycamores, from between which the Sun-god appeared daily, and found the entrance to the Sekhet Ȧaru or Elysian Fields. Chapter CX and its vignette of the Elysian Fields have already been described (see p. 31). Chapters CXI and CXII describe how Horus lost the sight of his eye temporarily through looking at Set under the form of a black pig, and Chapter CXIII refers to the legend of the drowning of Horus and the recovery of his body by Sebek the Crocodile-god. Chapter CXIV enabled the deceased to absorb the wisdom of Thoth and his Eight gods. Chapters CXV–CXXII made him lord of the Ṭuats of Memphis and Heliopolis, and supplied him with food, and Chapter CXXIII enabled him to identify himself with Thoth. Chapters CXXIV and CXXV, which treat of the Judgment, have already been described. Chapter CXXVI contains a prayer to the Four Holy Apes, Chapter CXXVII a hymn to the gods of the " Circles " in the Ṭuat, and Chapter CXXVIII a hymn to Osiris. Chapters CXXX and CXXXI secured for the deceased the use of the Boats of Sunrise and Sunset, and Chapter CXXXII enabled him to return to earth and visit the house he had lived in. Chapters CXXXIII (or CXXXIX)-CXXXVI resemble in contents Chapter CXXXI. Chapter CXXXVII describes a series of magical ceremonies that were to be performed for the deceased daily in order to make him to become a "living soul for ever." The formulae are said to have been composed under the IVth dynasty. Chapter CXXXVIII refers to the ceremony of reconstituting Osiris, and Chapters CXL-CXLII deal with the setting up of twelve altars, and the making of offerings to all the gods and to the various forms of Osiris. Chapter CXLIII consists of a series of vignettes, in three of which solar boats are represented.

Chapters CXLIV and CXLVII deal with the Seven Great Halls (*Árit*) of the Kingdom of Osiris. The gate of each Hall was guarded by a porter, a watchman, and a messenger ; the first kept the door, the second looked out for the arrival of visitors, and the third took their names to Osiris. No one could enter a Hall without repeating the name of it, of the porter, of the watchman, and of the messenger. According to a late tradition the Gates of the Kingdom of Osiris were twenty-one in number (Chapters CXLV and CXLVI), and each had a magical name, and each was guarded by one or two gods, whose names had to be repeated by the deceased before he could pass. Chapter CXLVIII supplied the deceased with the names of the Seven Cows and their Bull on which the "gods" were supposed to feed. Chapters CXLIX and CL give the names of the Fourteen Áats, or districts, of the Kingdom of Osiris. Chapter CLIA and CLIB give a picture of the mummy chamber and the magical texts that were necessary for the protection of both the chamber and the mummy in it. Chapter CLII provided a house for the deceased in the Celestial Ánu, and Chapter CLIIIA and CLIIIB enabled his soul to avoid capture in the net of the snarer of souls. Chapter CLIV is an address to Osiris in which the deceased says, "I shall not decay, nor rot, nor putrefy, nor "become worms, nor see corruption. I shall have my being, "I shall live, I shall flourish, I shall rise up in peace." Chapters CLV-CLXVII are spells which were engraved on the amulets 𓊽, 𓊾, 𓄤, 𓊽, 𓏴, 𓄂, etc., giving the deceased the protection of Rã, Osiris, Isis, Horus, and 6ther gods. The remaining Chapters (CLXVIII-CXC) are of a miscellaneous character, and few of them are found in more than one or two papyri of the Book of the Dead. A few contain hymns that are not older than the XVIIIth dynasty, and one is an extract from the text on the Pyramid of Unâs (lines 379–399). The most interesting is, perhaps, Chapter CLXXV, which describes the Ṭuat as airless, waterless, and lightless. In this chapter the deceased is assured of immortailty in the words, "Thou shalt live for millions of millions of years, a life of millions of years."

E. A. WALLIS BUDGE.

DEPARTMENT OF EGYPTIAN AND ASSYRIAN
ANTIQUITIES, BRITISH MUSEUM.
April 15, 1920.

NOTE.

The Trustees of the British Museum have published :—

1. Coloured facsimile of the Papyrus of Hunefer, XIXth dynasty, with hieroglyphic transcript and translation. 11 plates, large folio.

2. Coloured facsimile of the Papyrus of Ȧnhai, XXIst dynasty, with hieroglyphic transcript and translation. 8 plates, large folio.

3. Collotype reproduction of the Papyrus of Queen Netchemet, XXIst dynasty, with hieroglyphic transcript and translation. 12 plates, large folio.

4. Coloured reproduction of the hieratic text of the Book of Breathings, with hieroglyphic transcript and translation. With 2 collotypes of the vignettes, large folio.

5. Hieroglyphic transcript of the Papyrus of Nu, with one collotype plate.

Nos. 1-5 are bound in one volume, price £2 10s.

6. Collotype reproduction of the Papyrus of Queen Nesita-nebt-ashru, with full descriptions of the vignettes, translations, and introduction, containing several illustrations, and 116 plates of hieratic text. Large 4to. Price £2 10s.